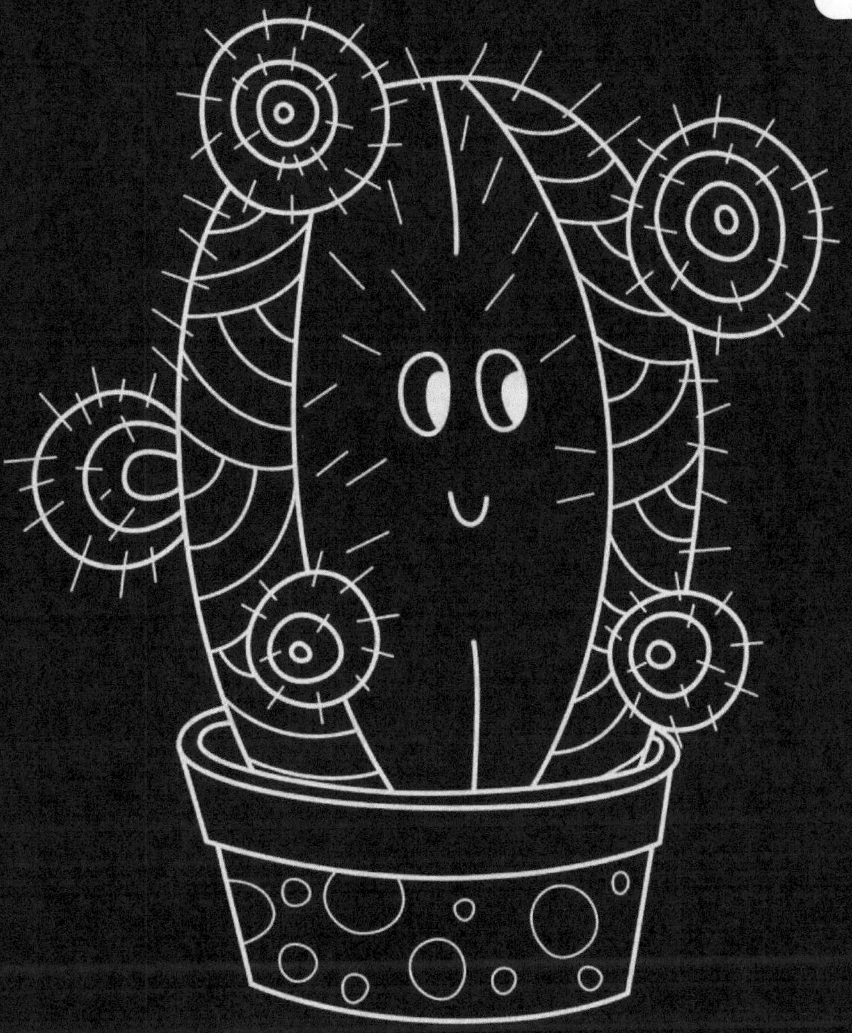

# TINY CACTUS PUBLISHING

CLORIST NAME

# TEST PAGE

PREPARE YOUR COLOR

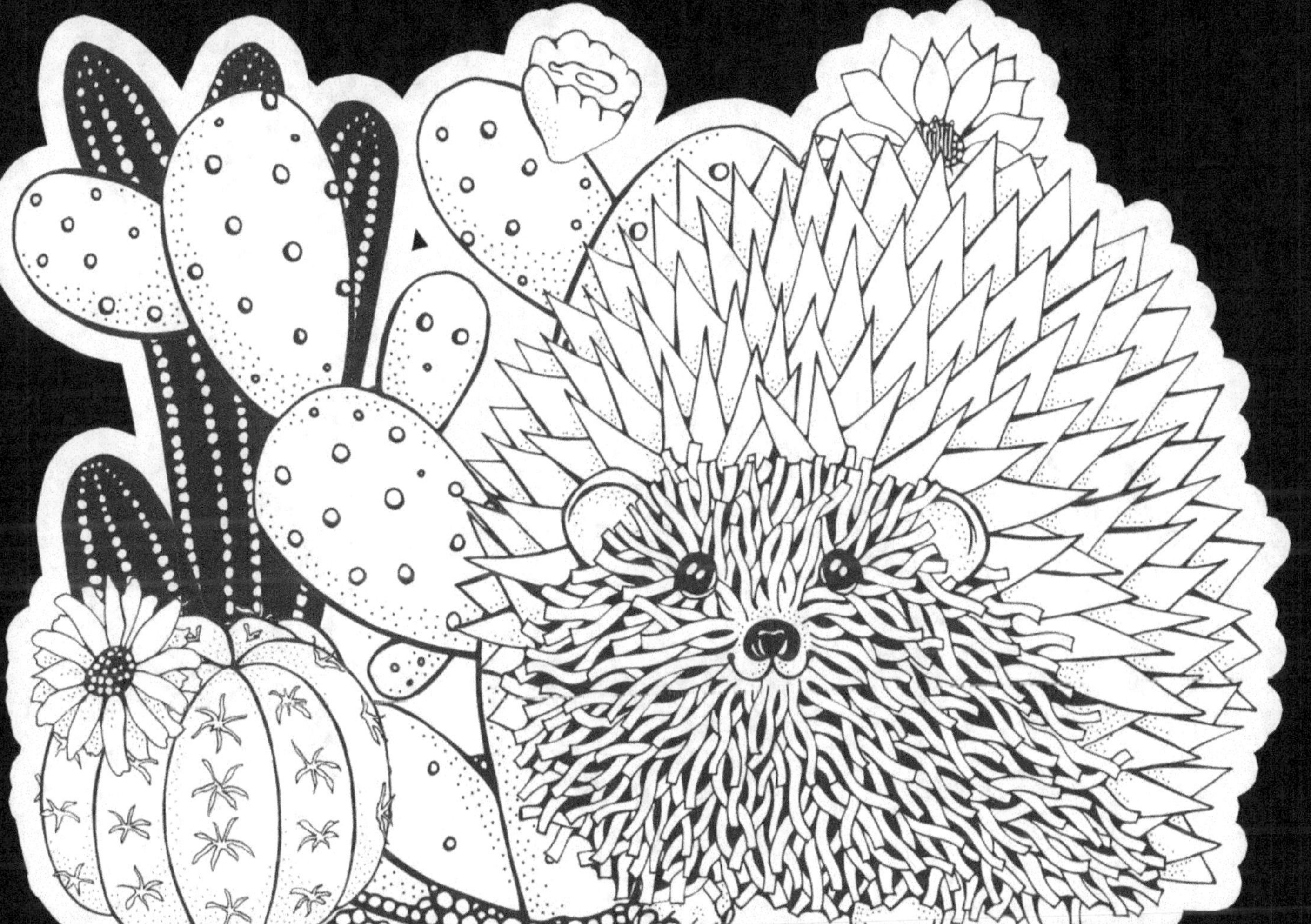

WARM UP !!

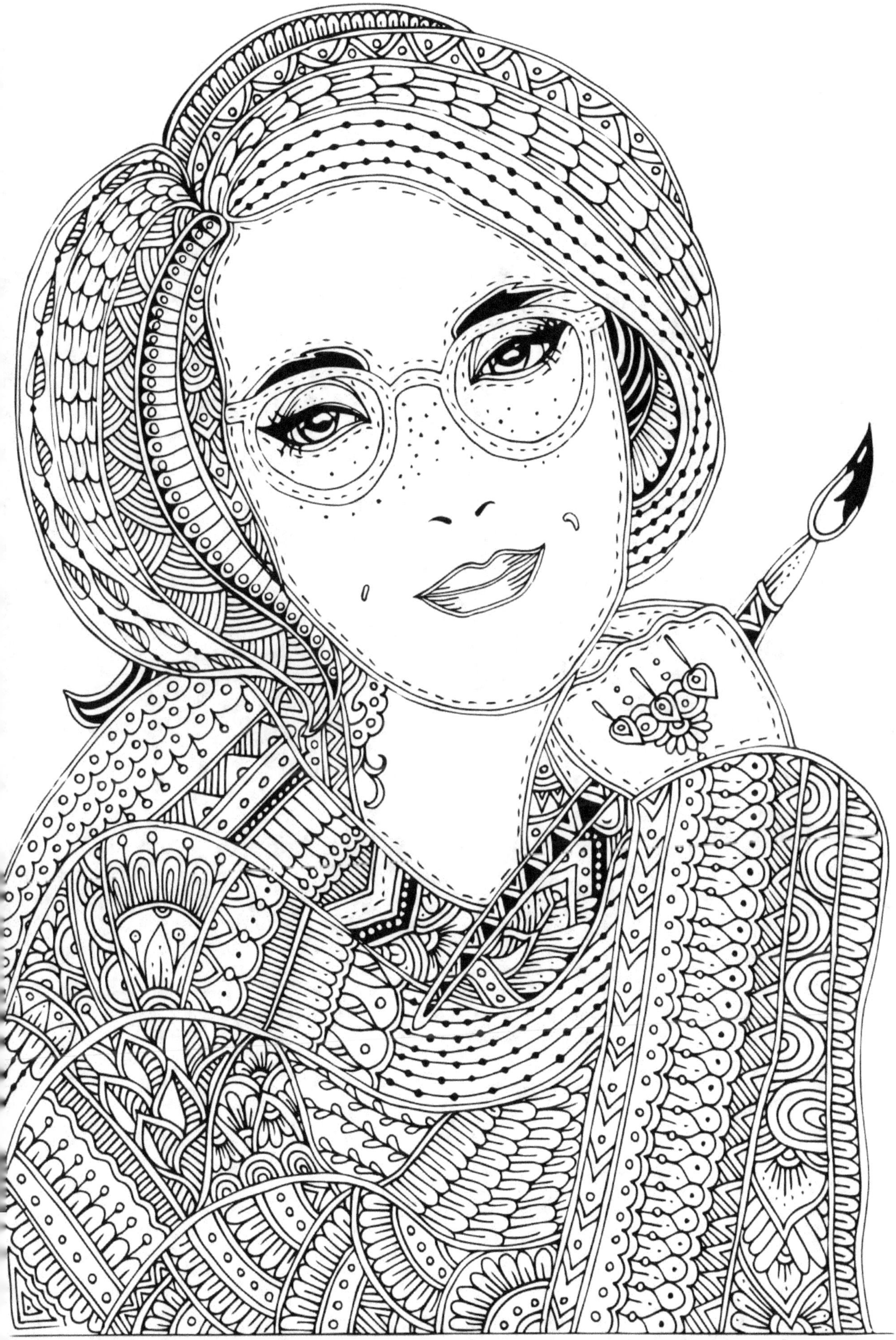

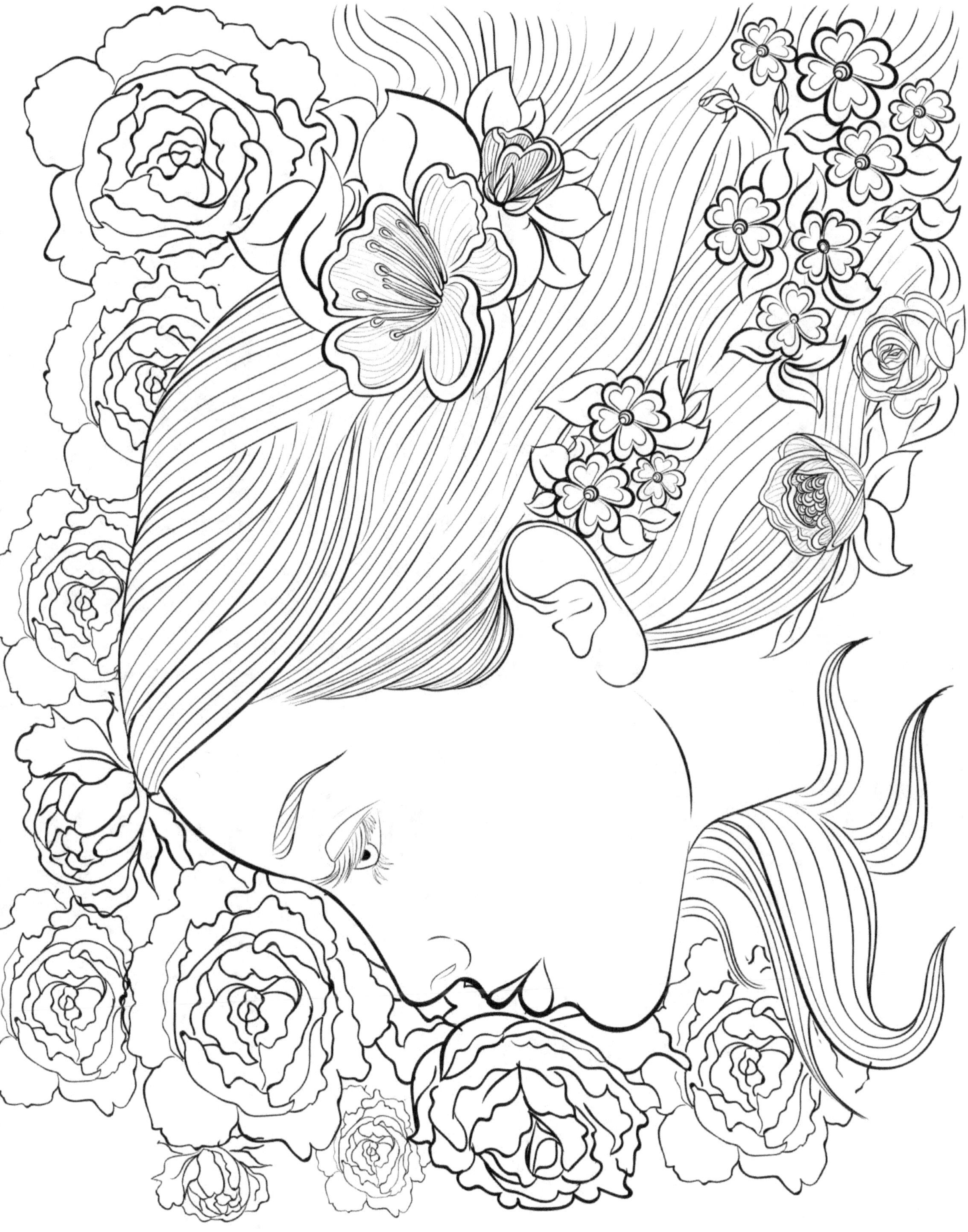

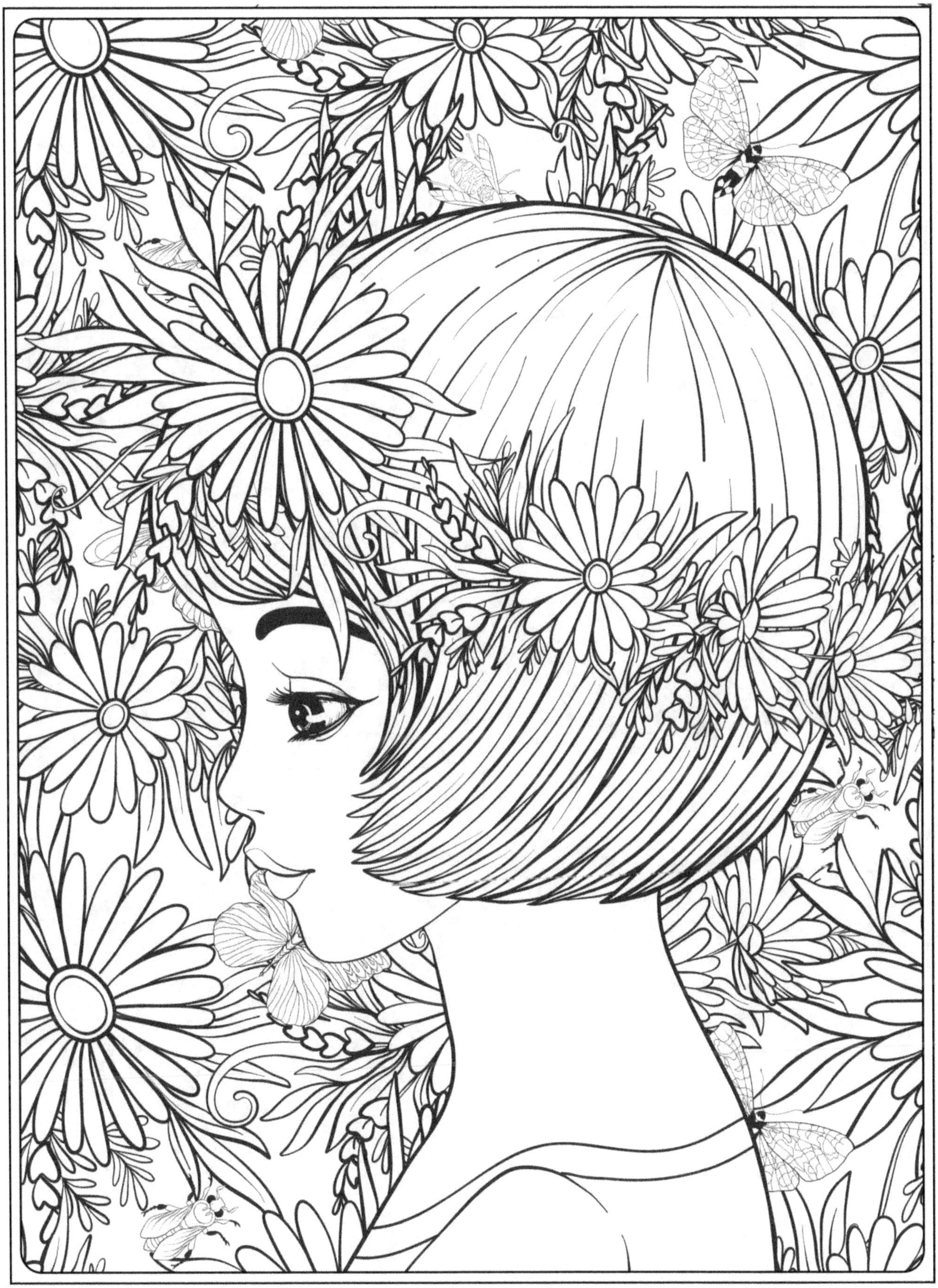

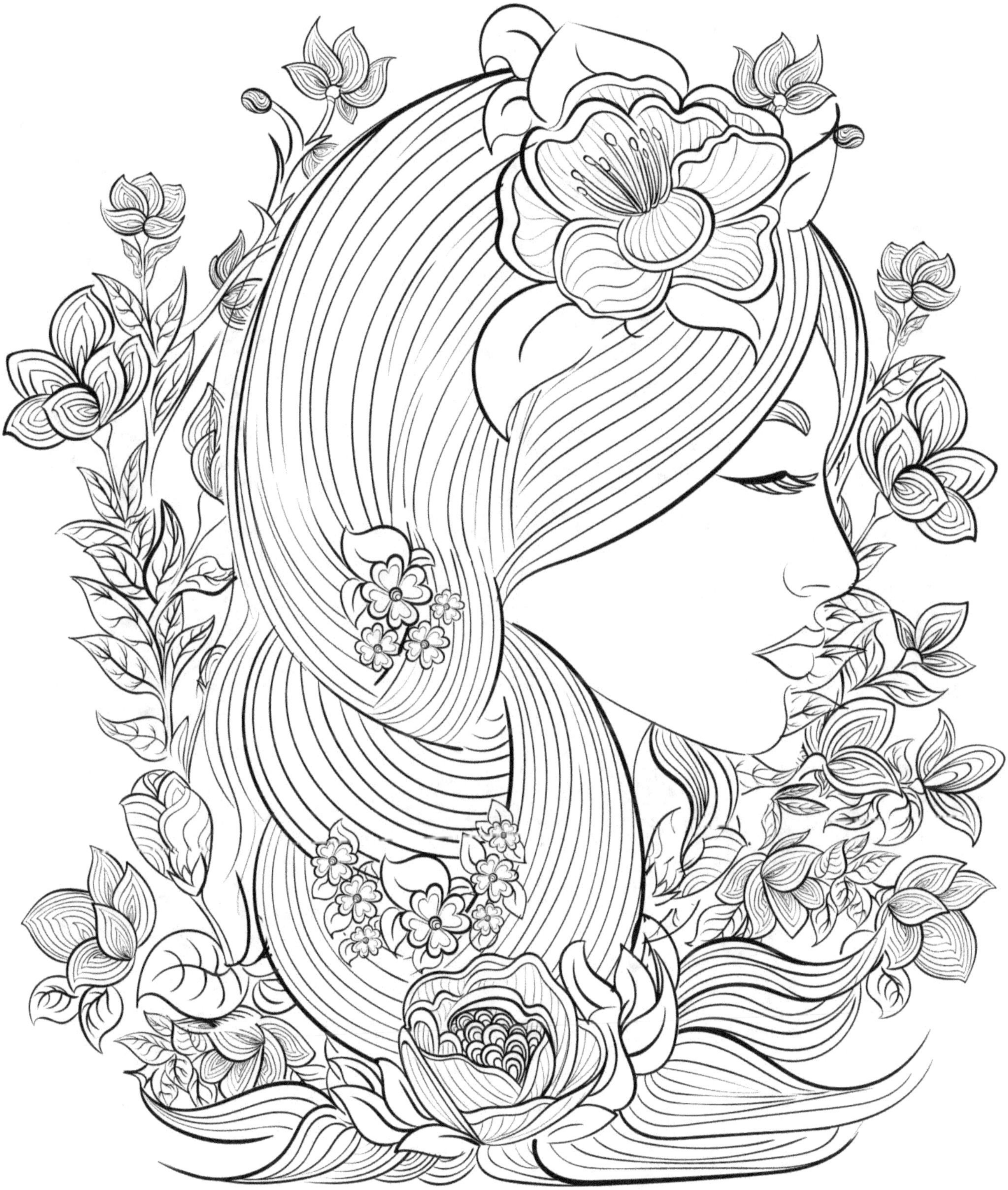

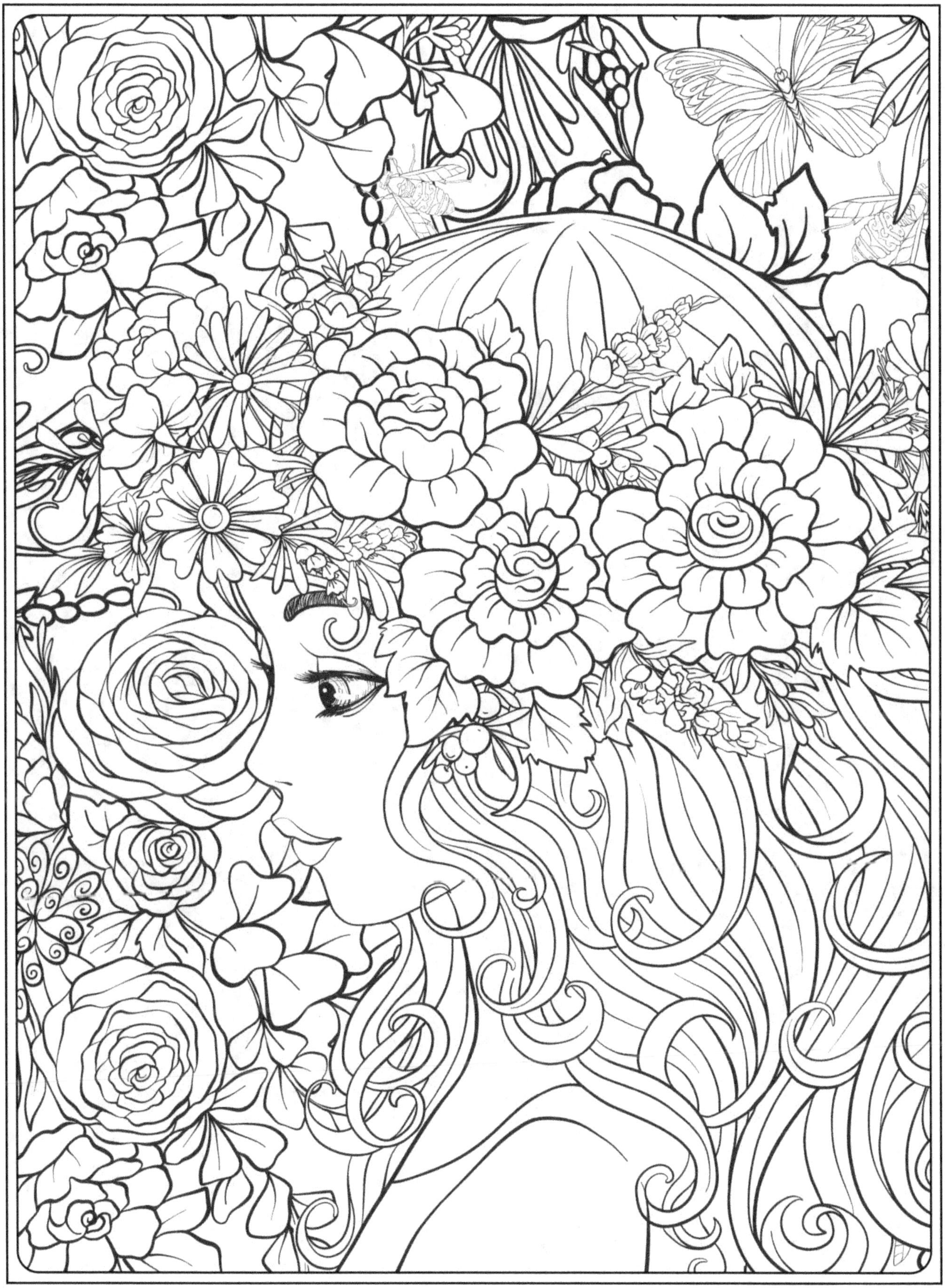

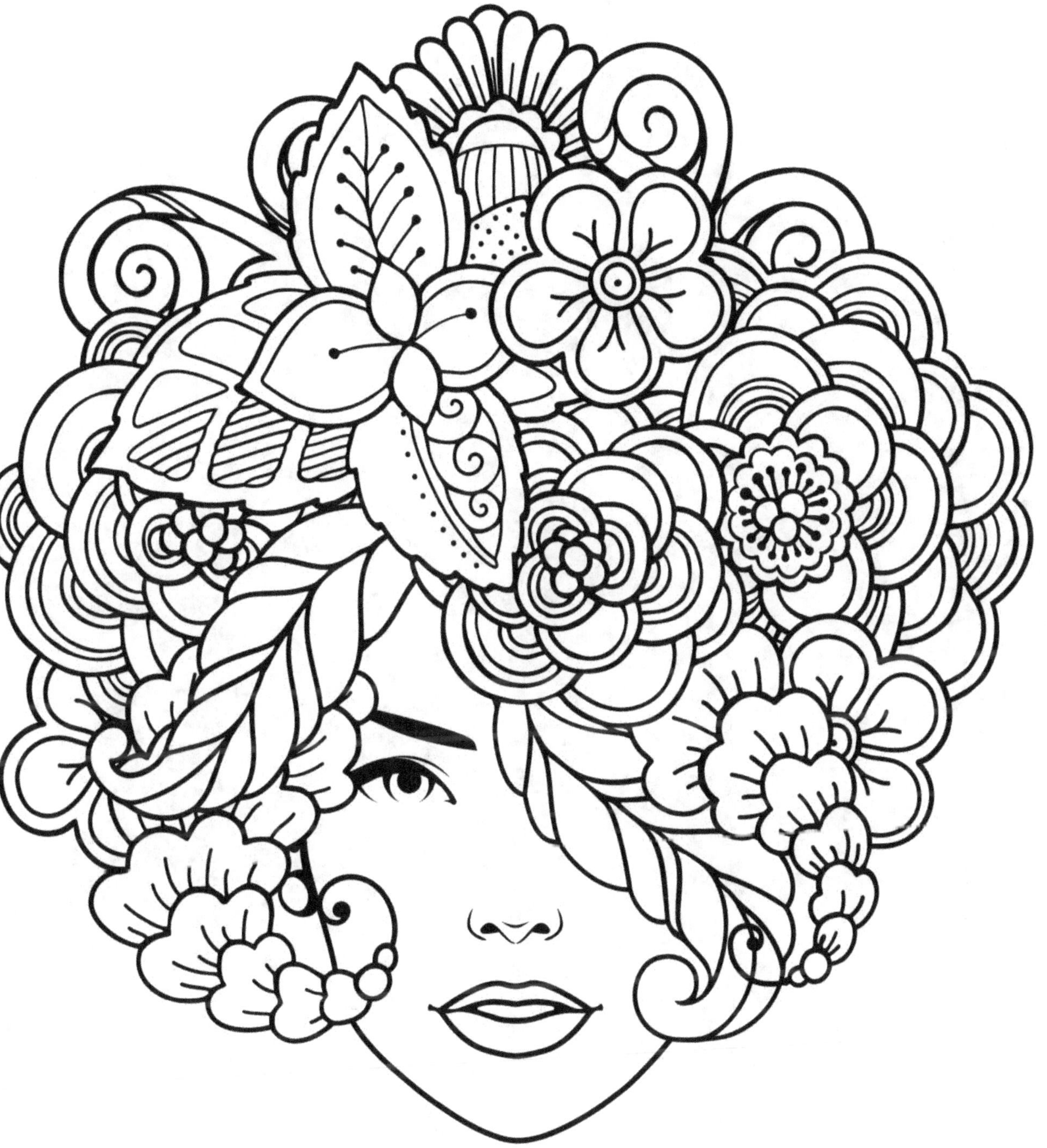

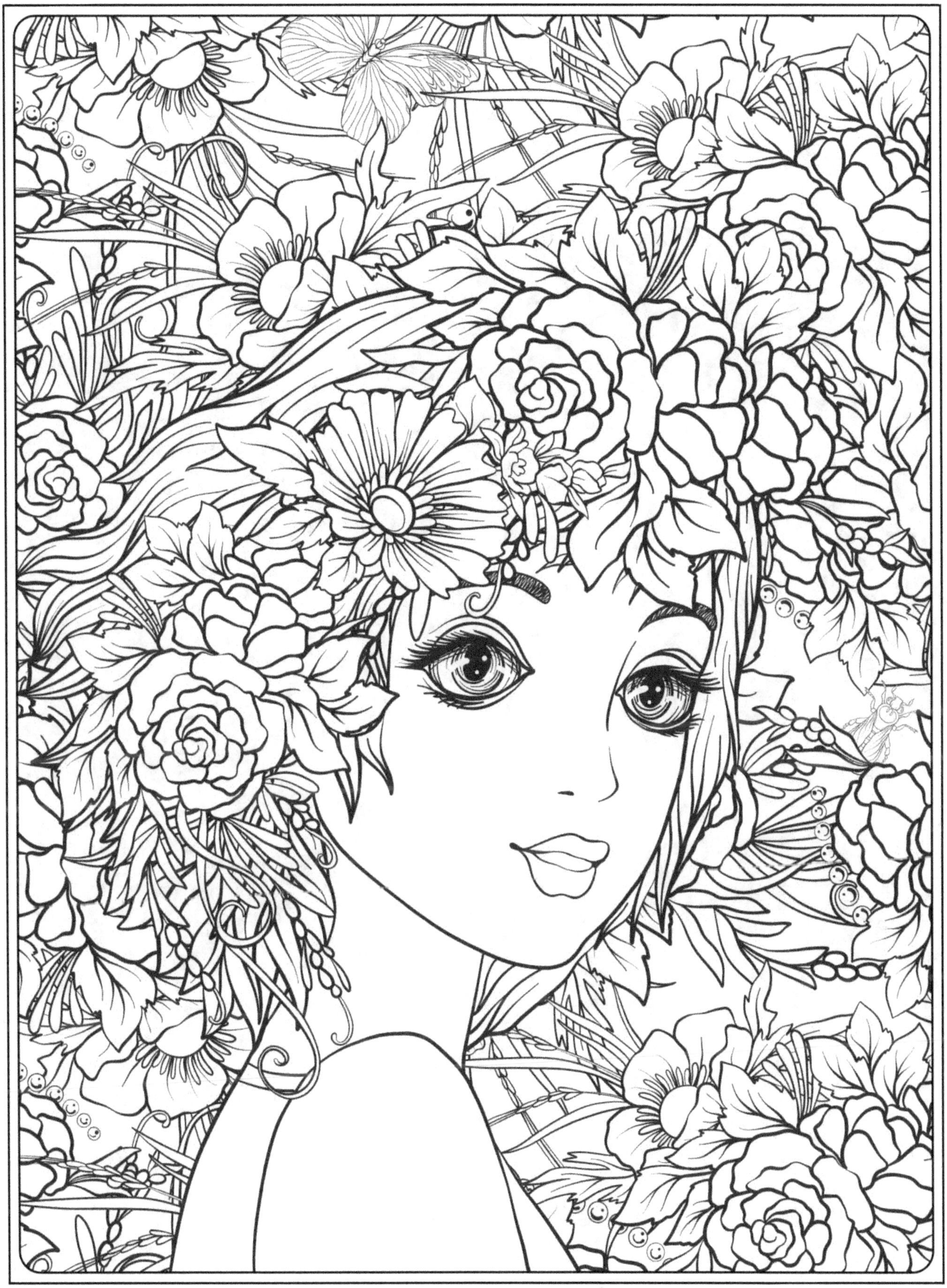

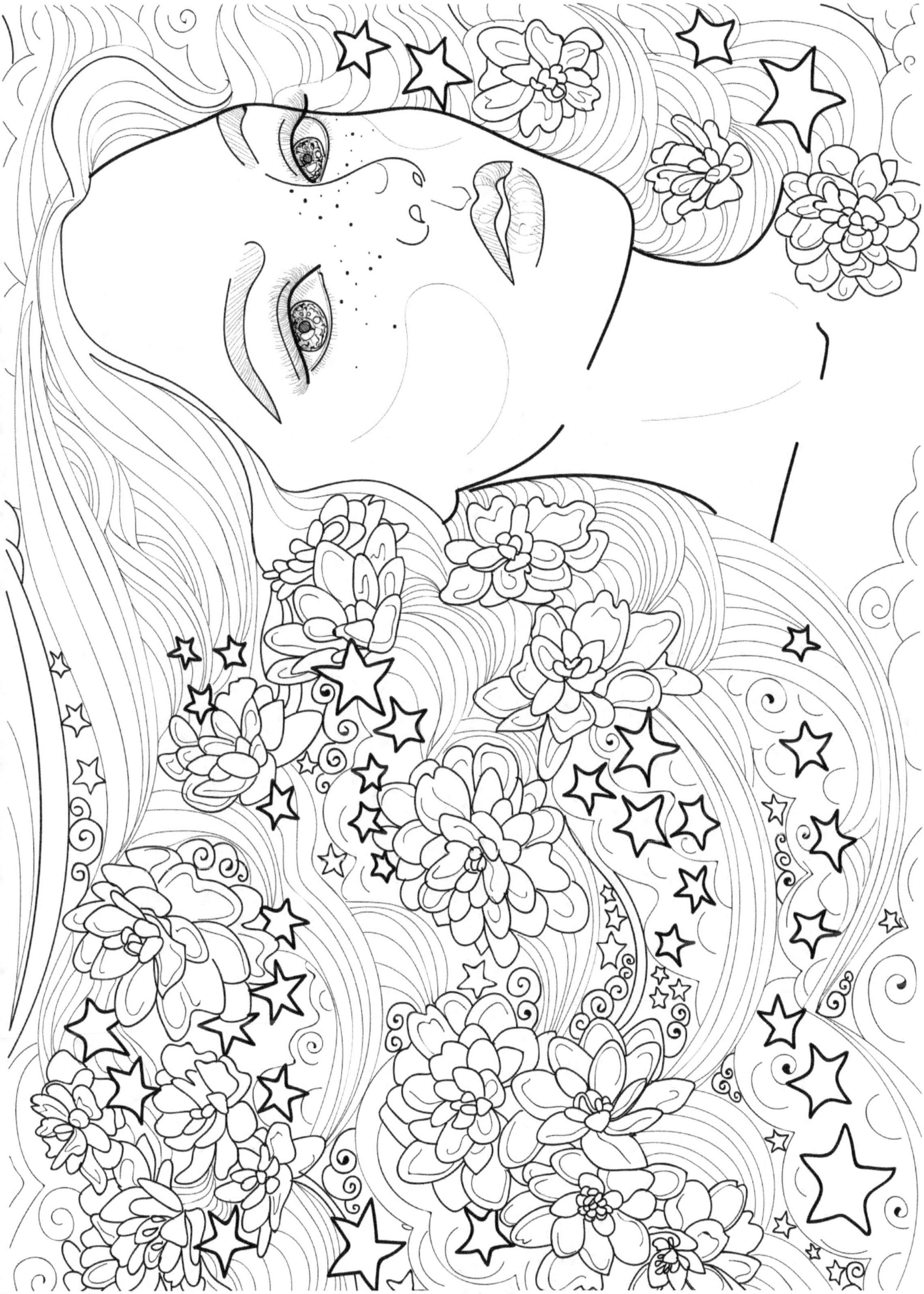

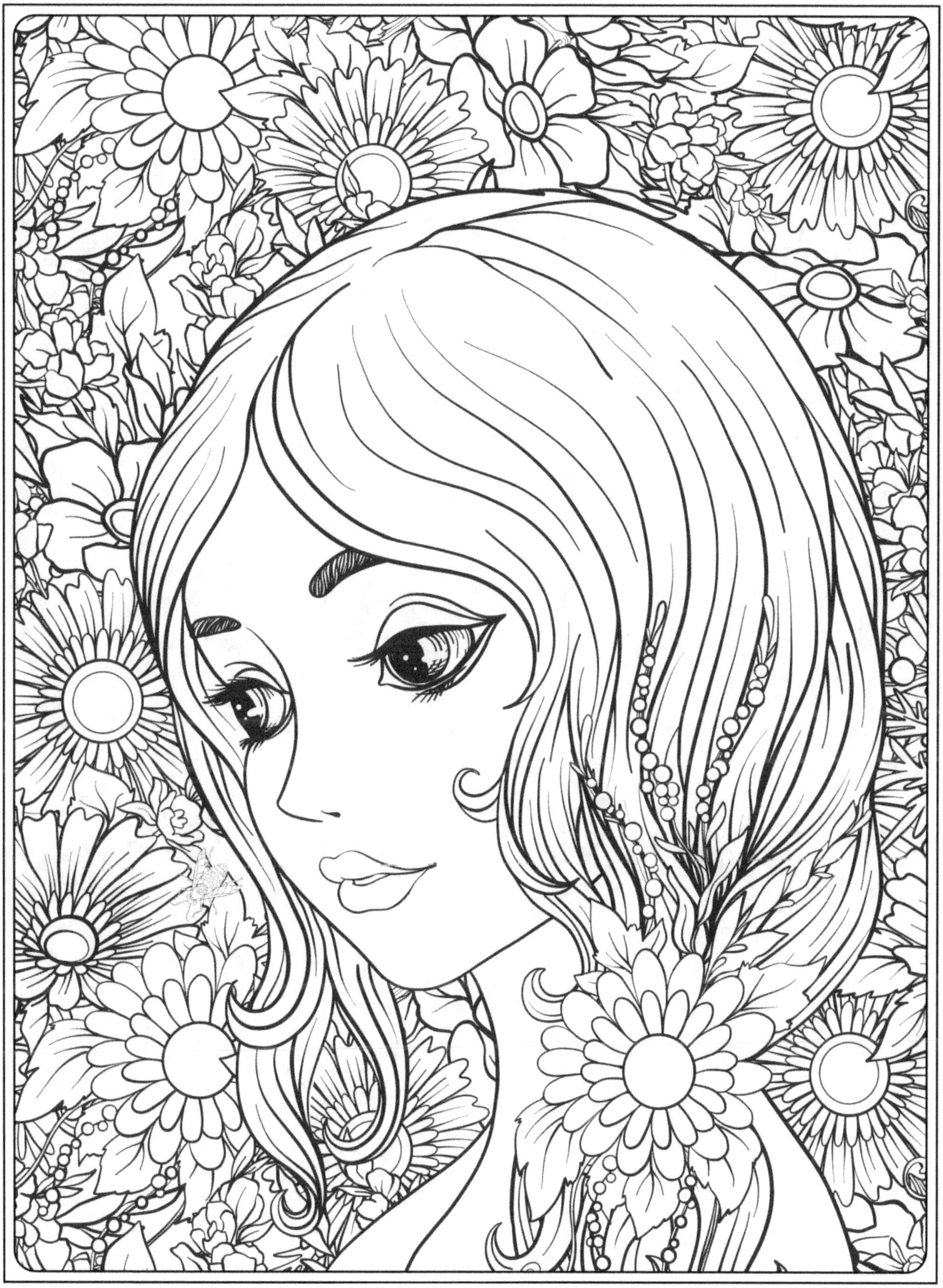

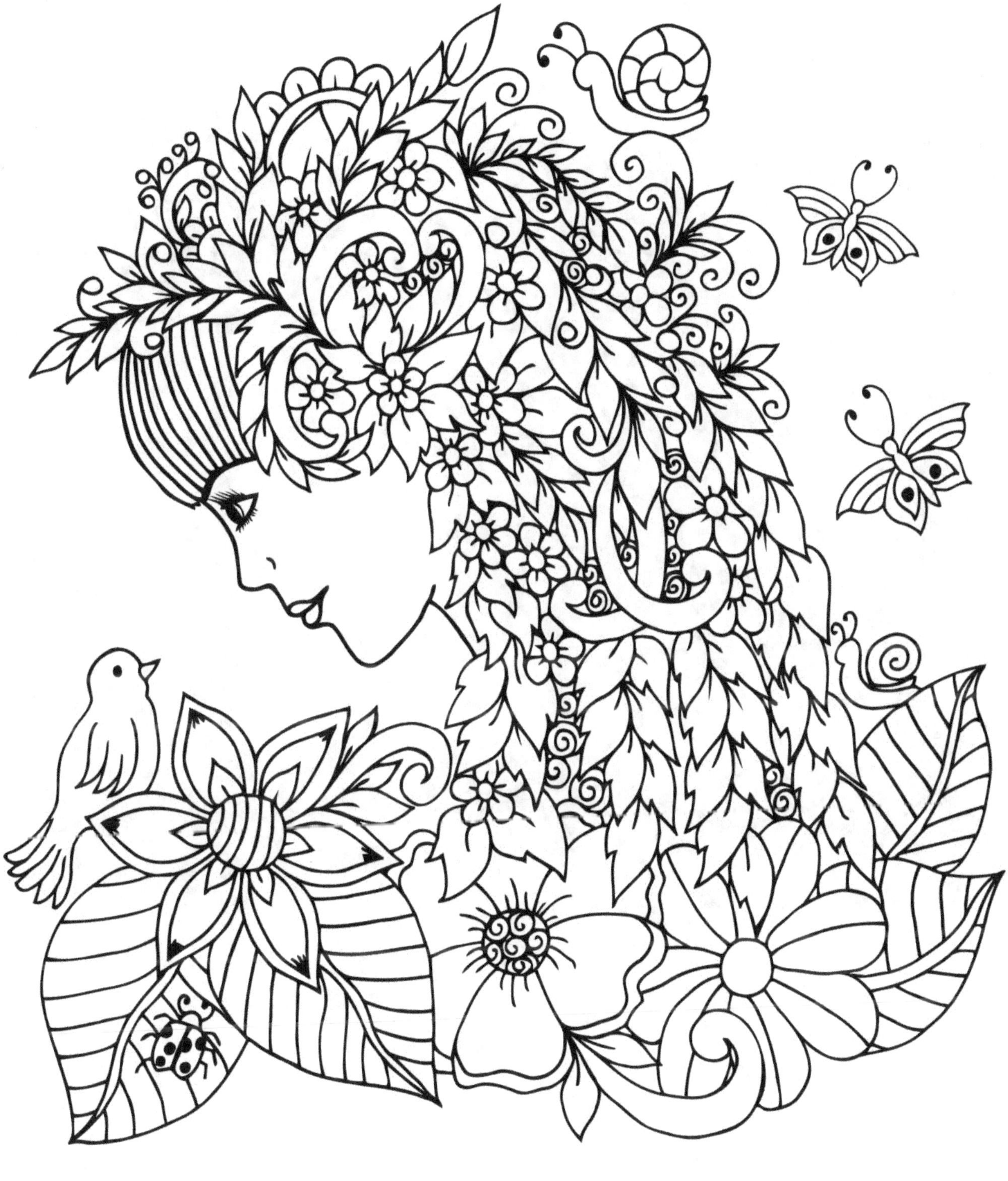

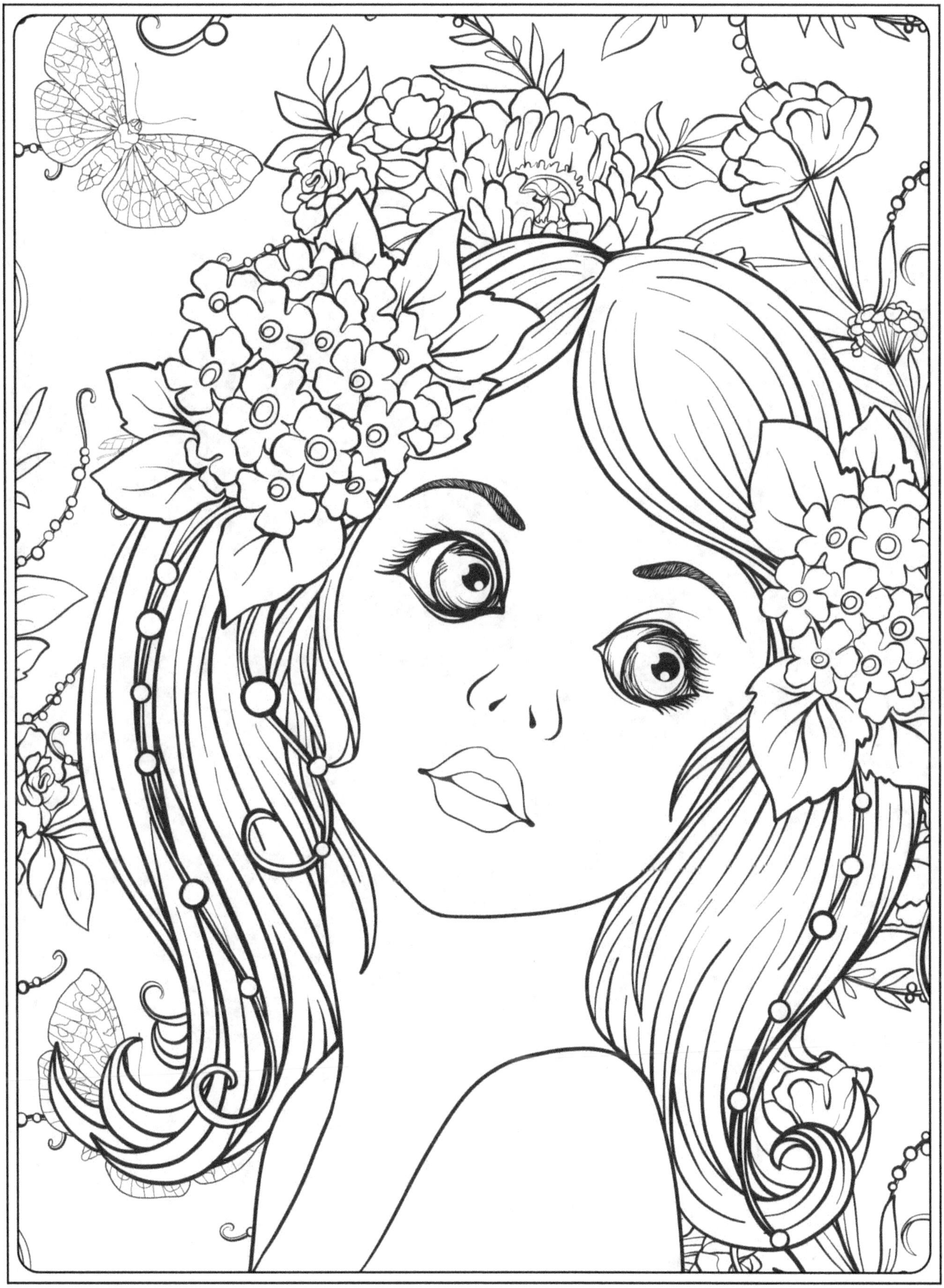

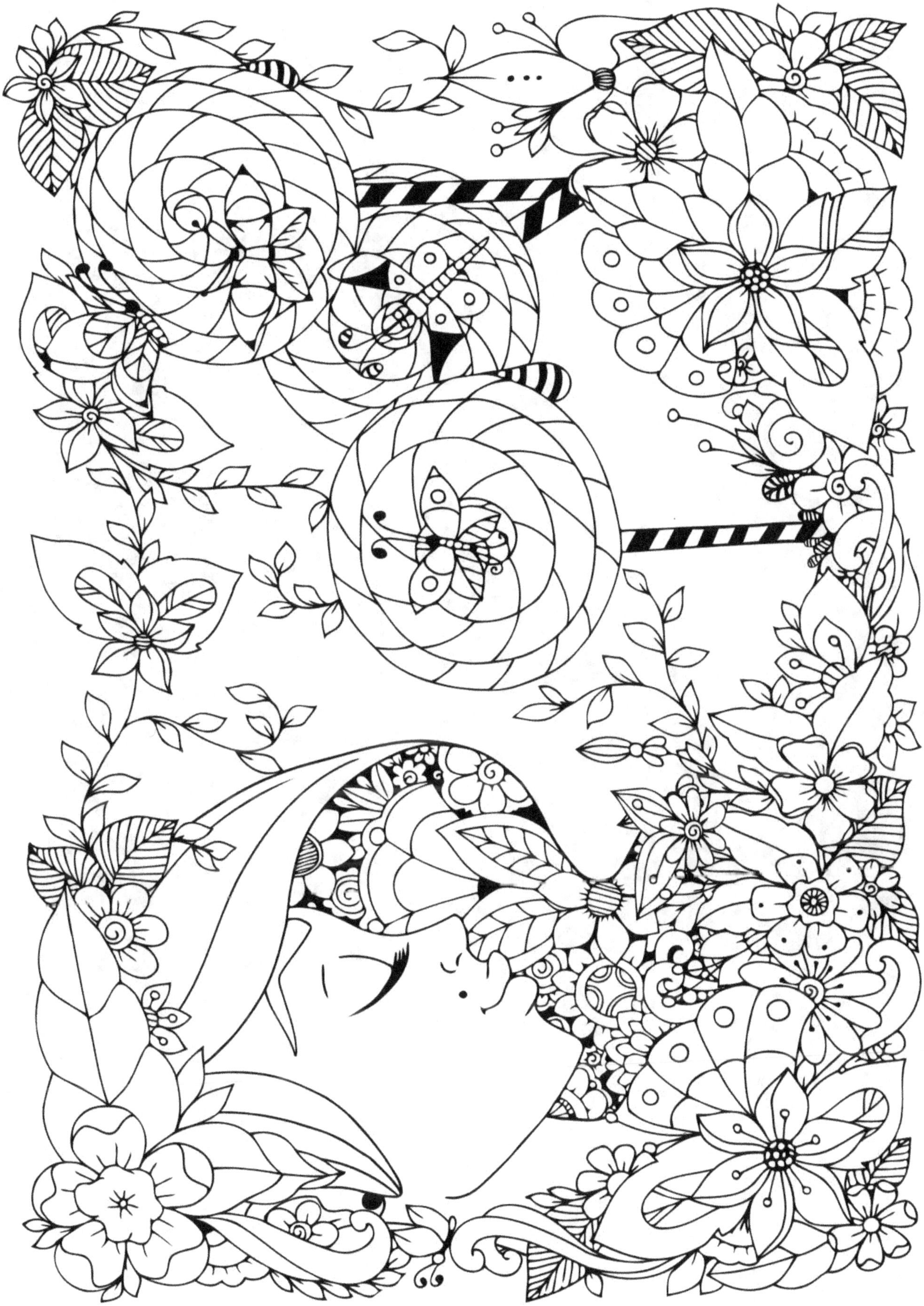

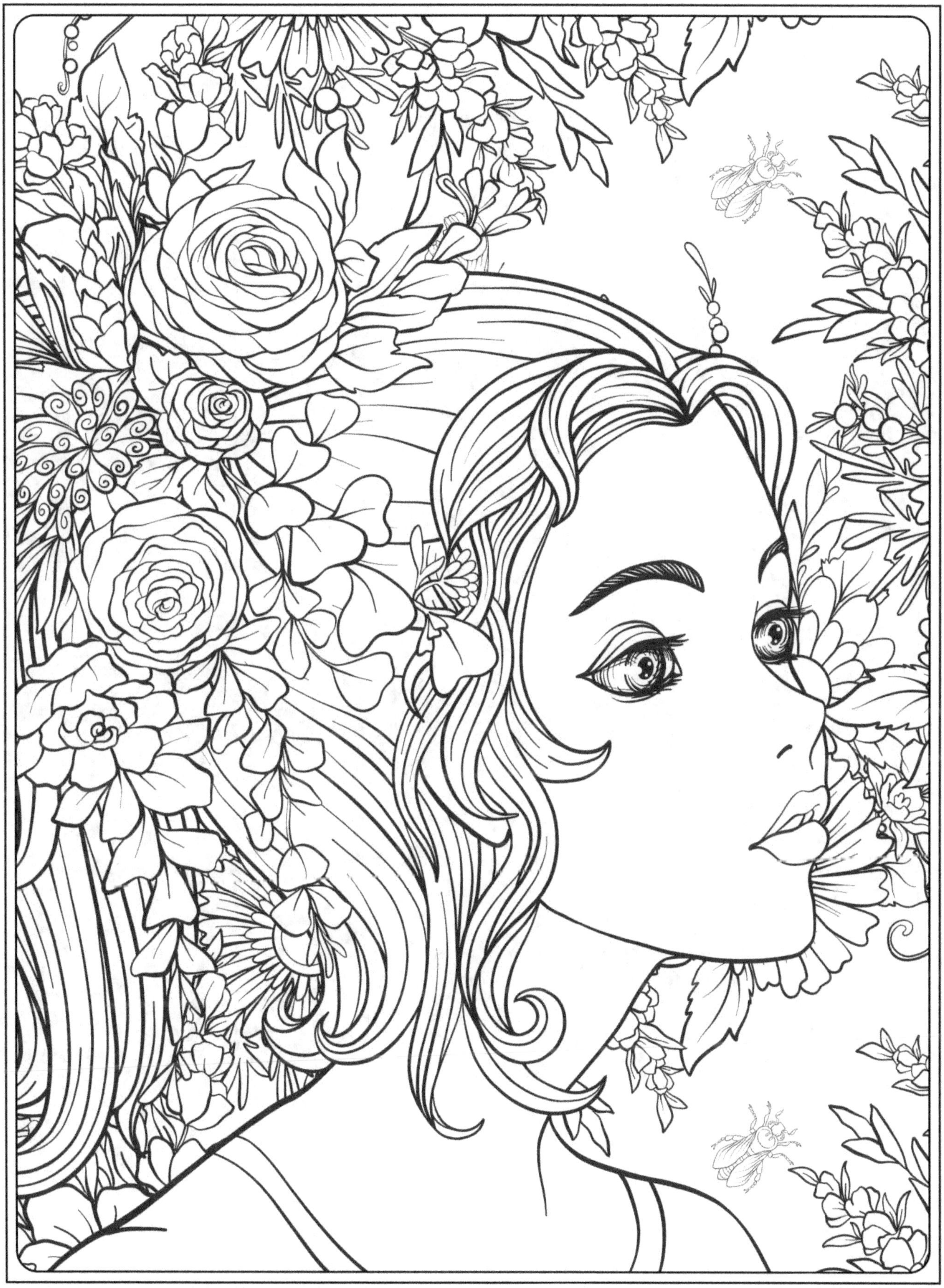

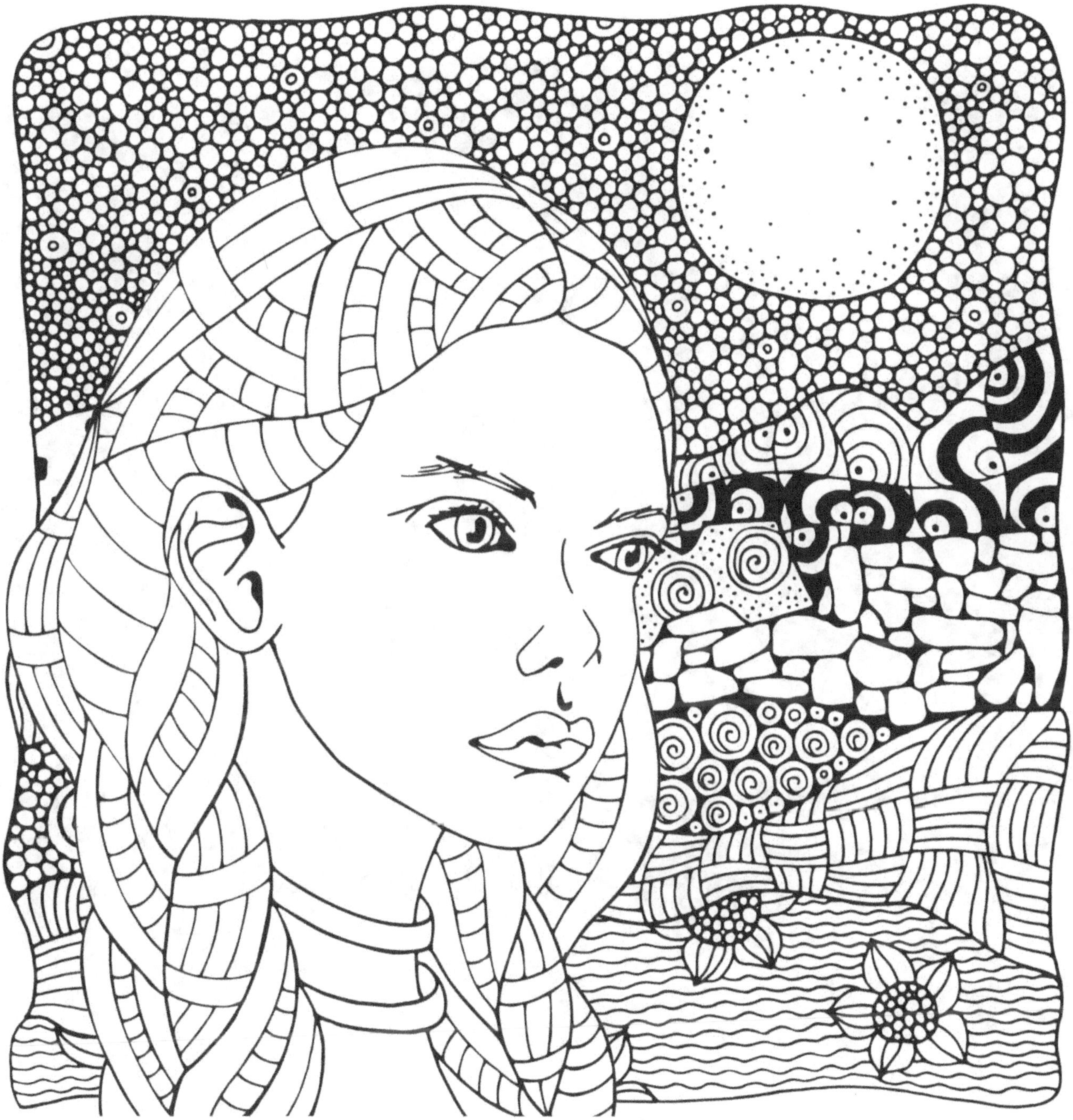

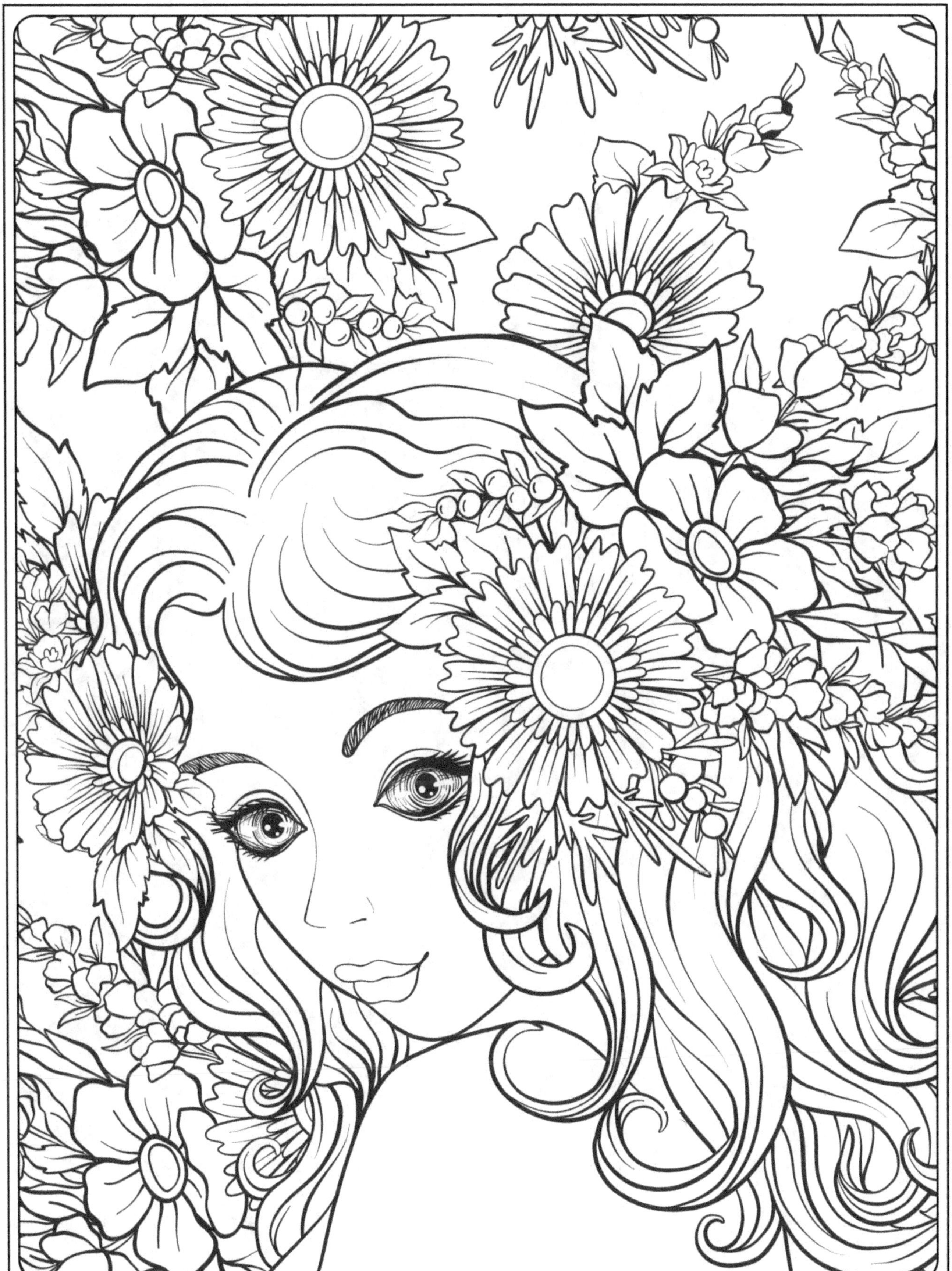

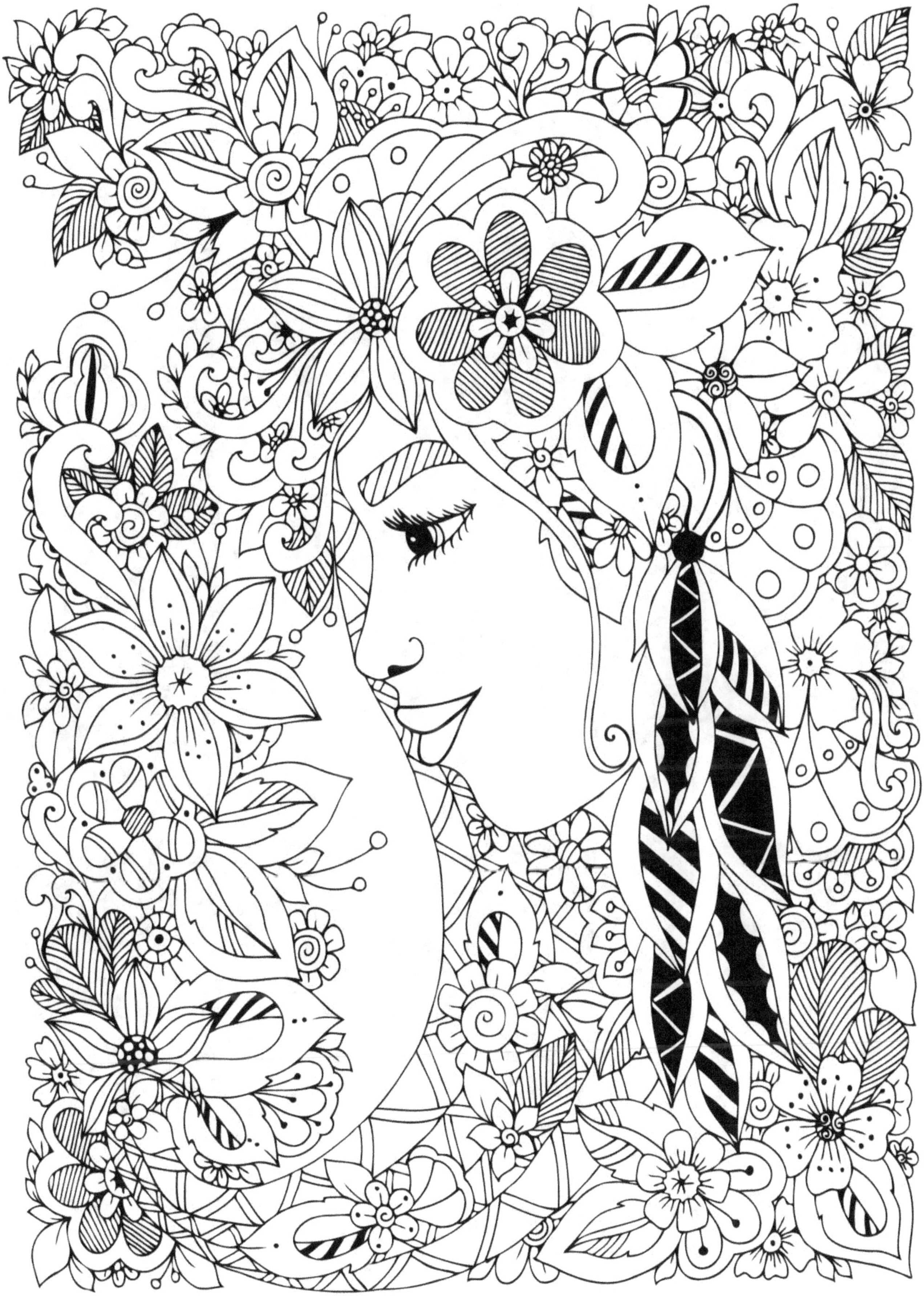

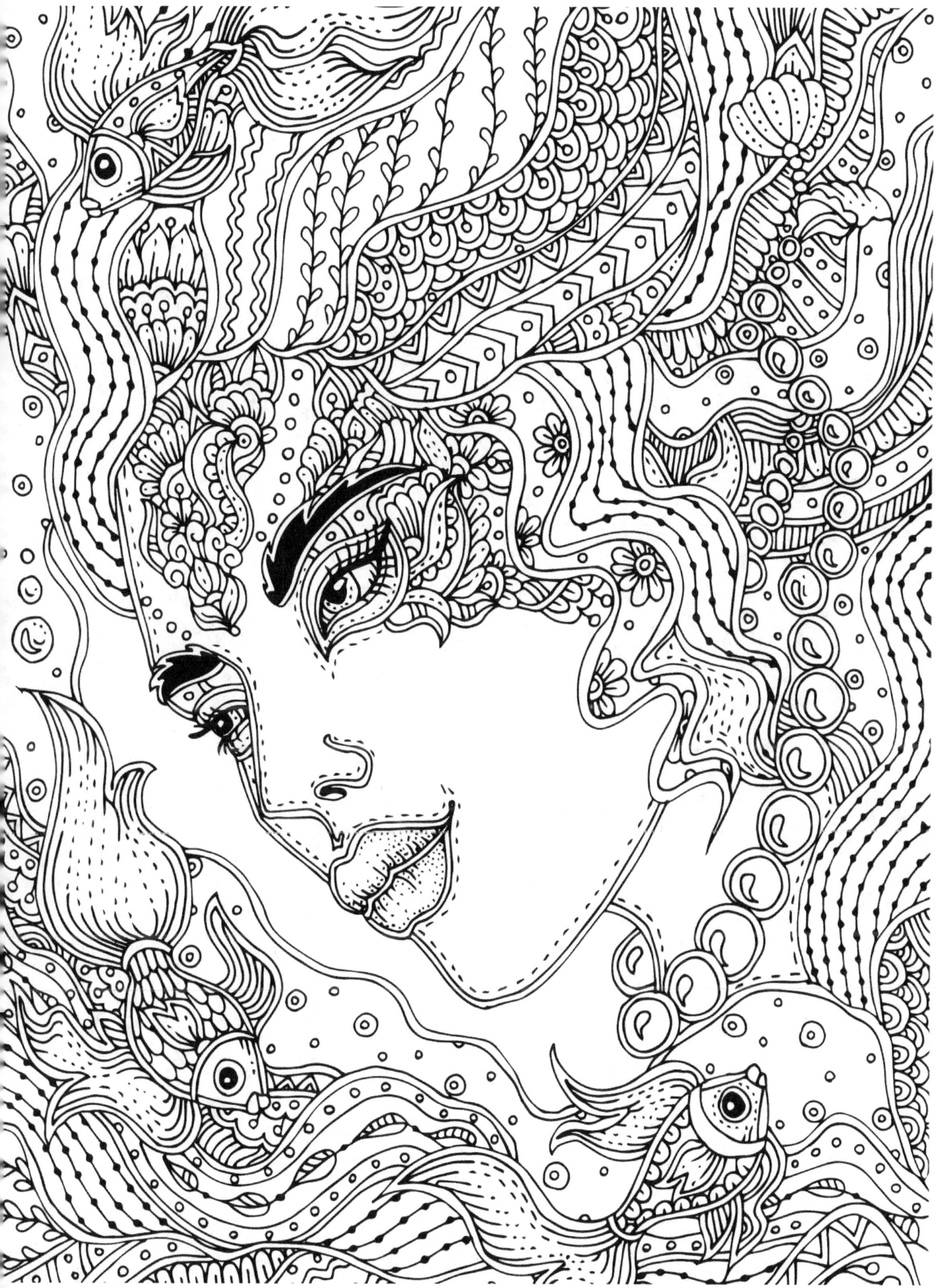

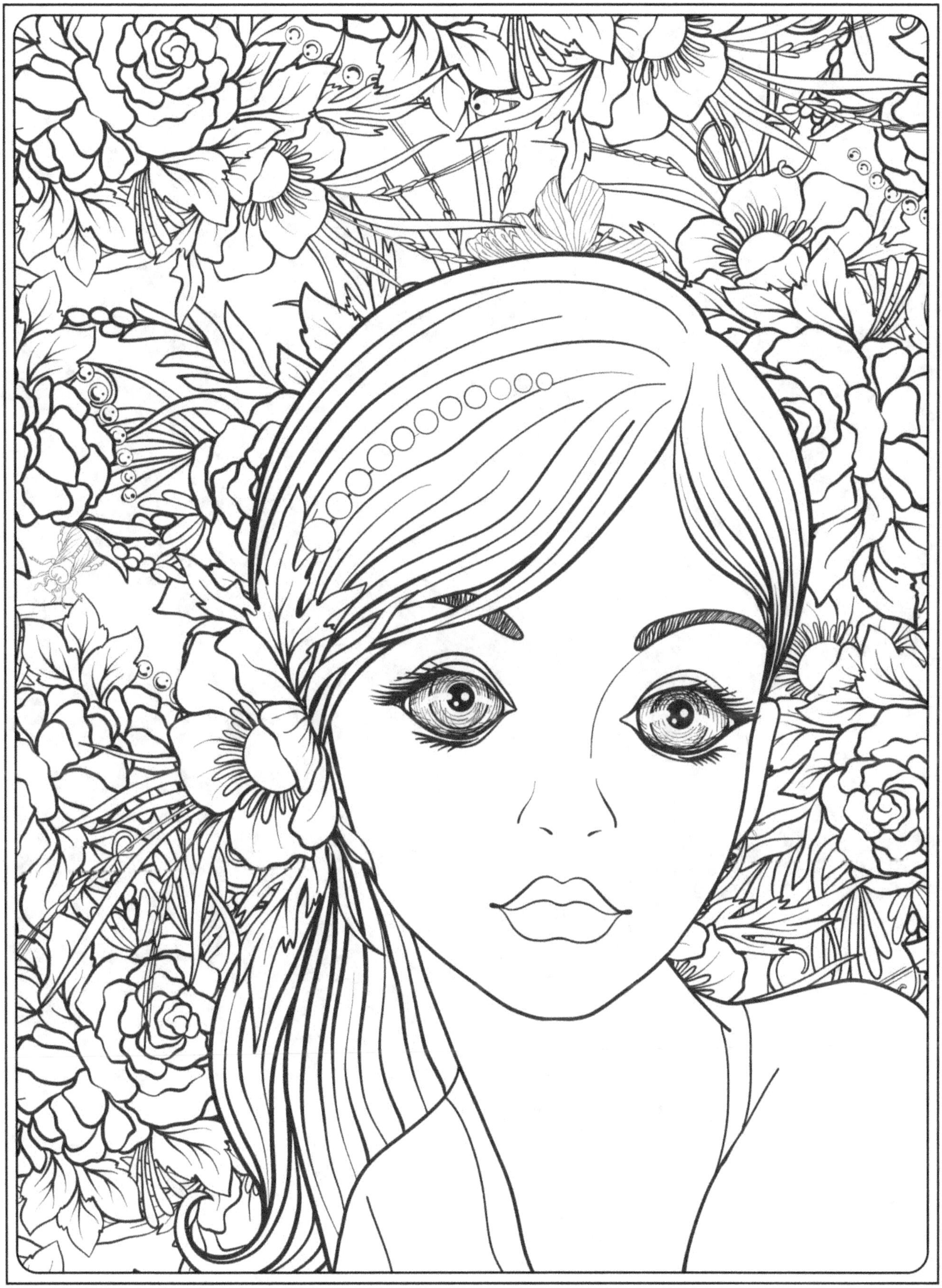

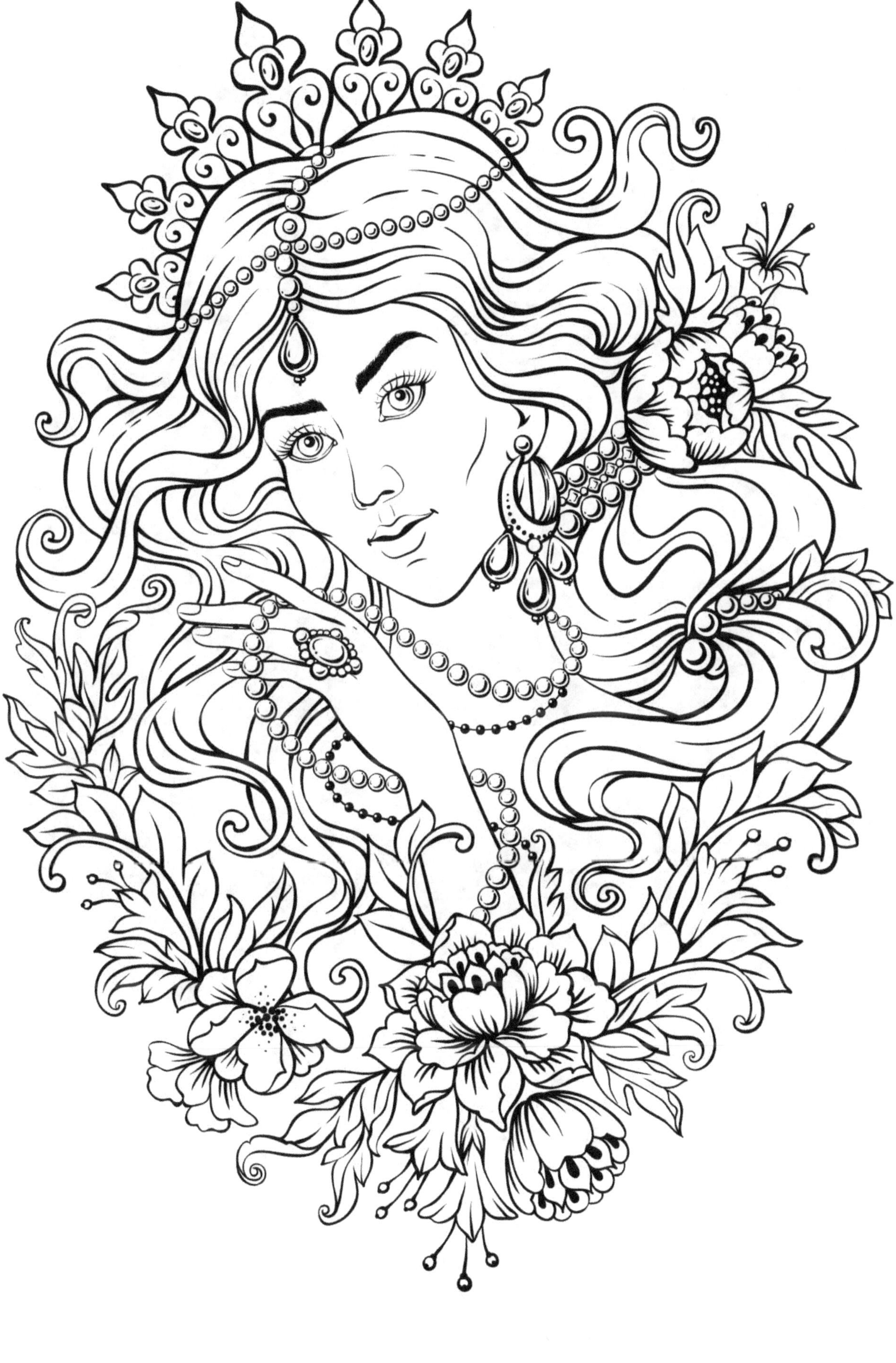

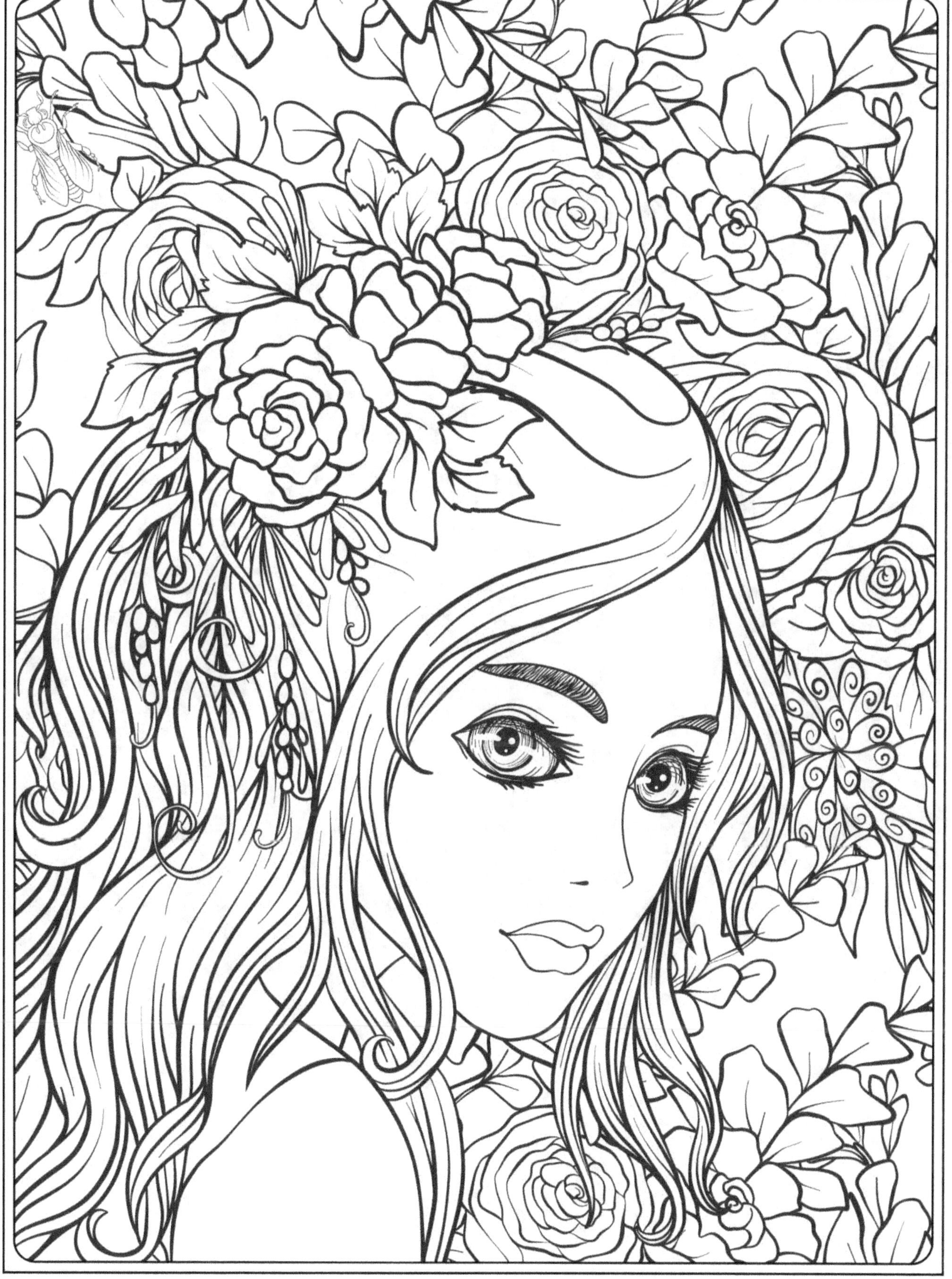

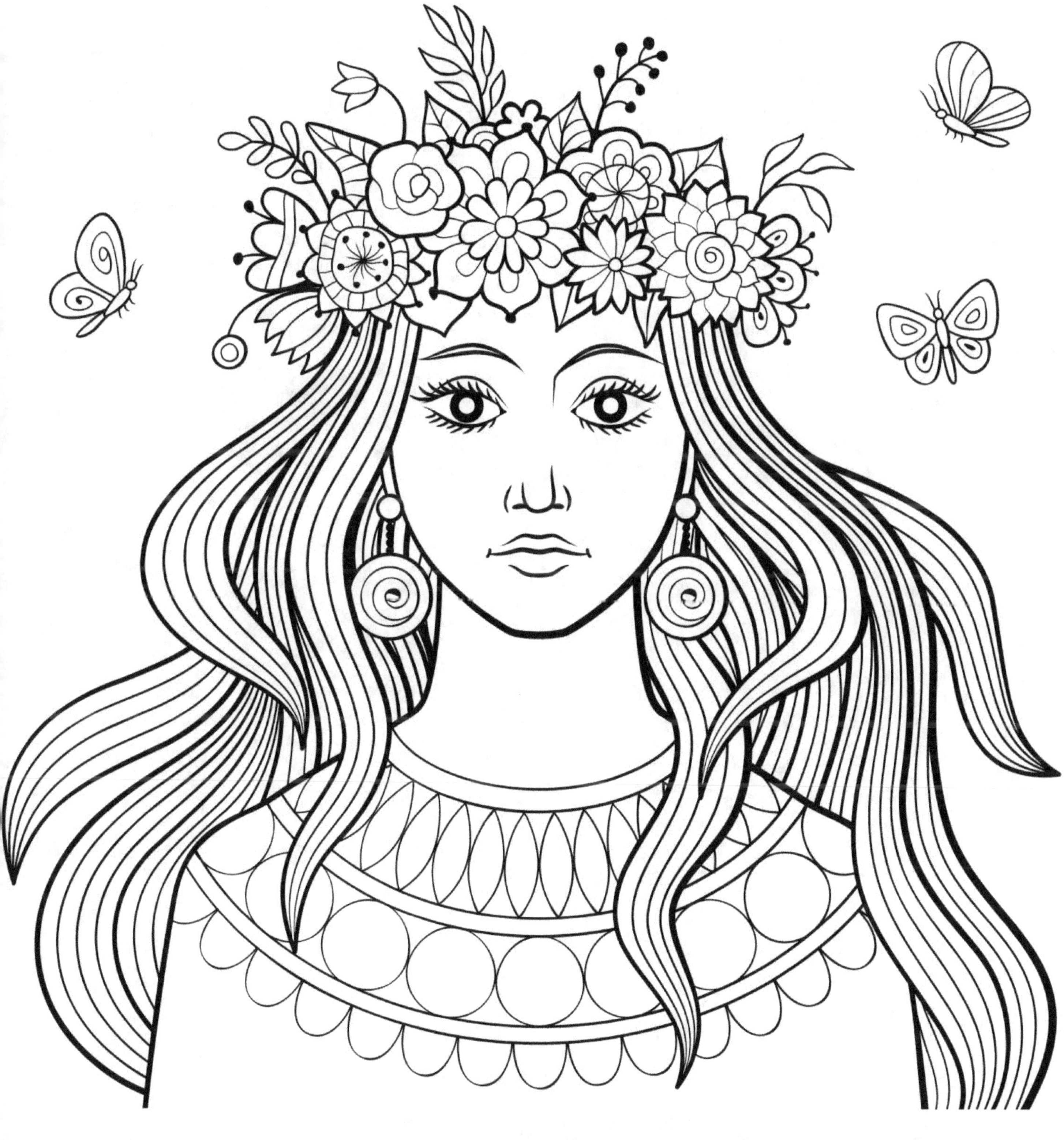

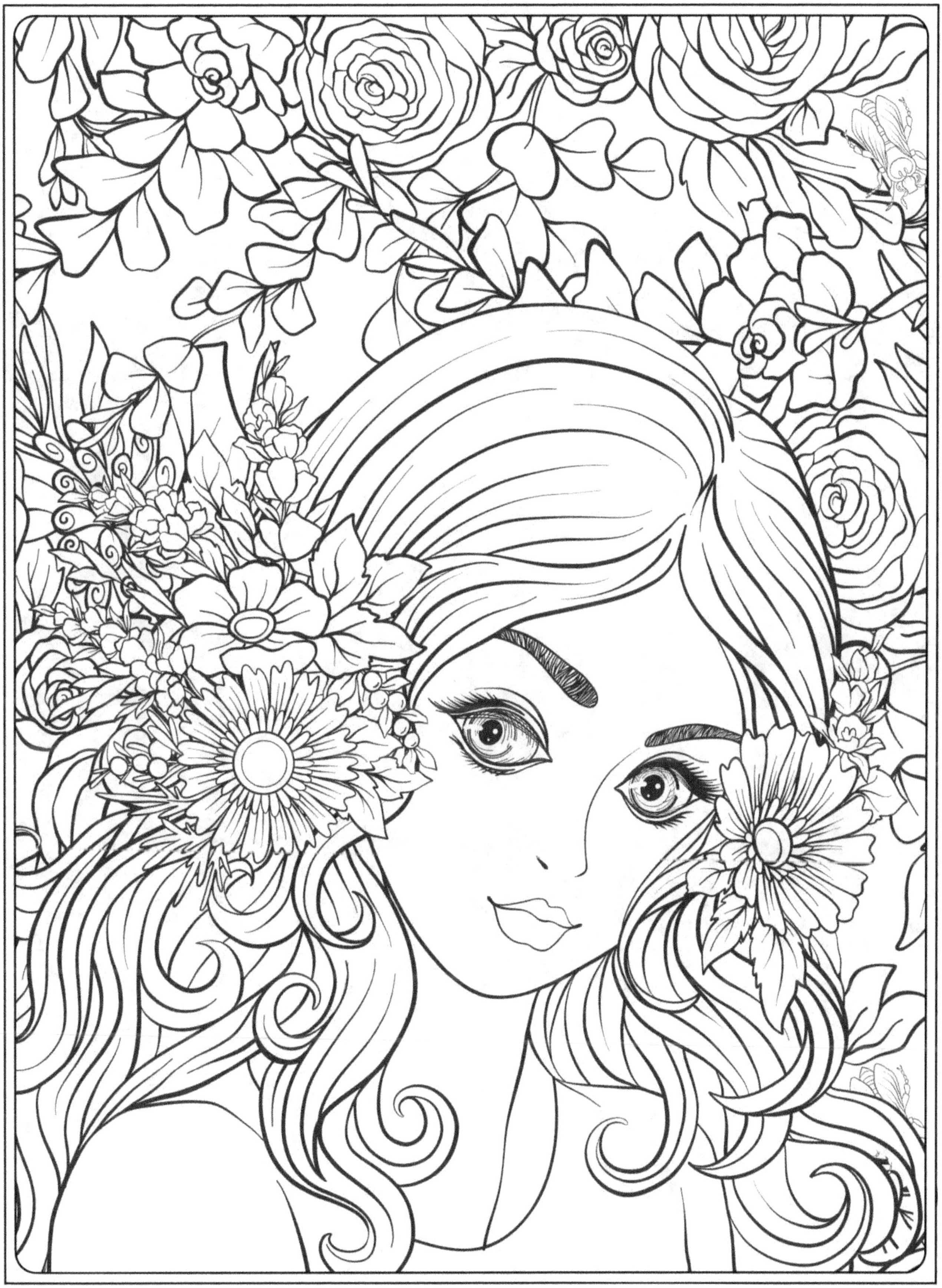

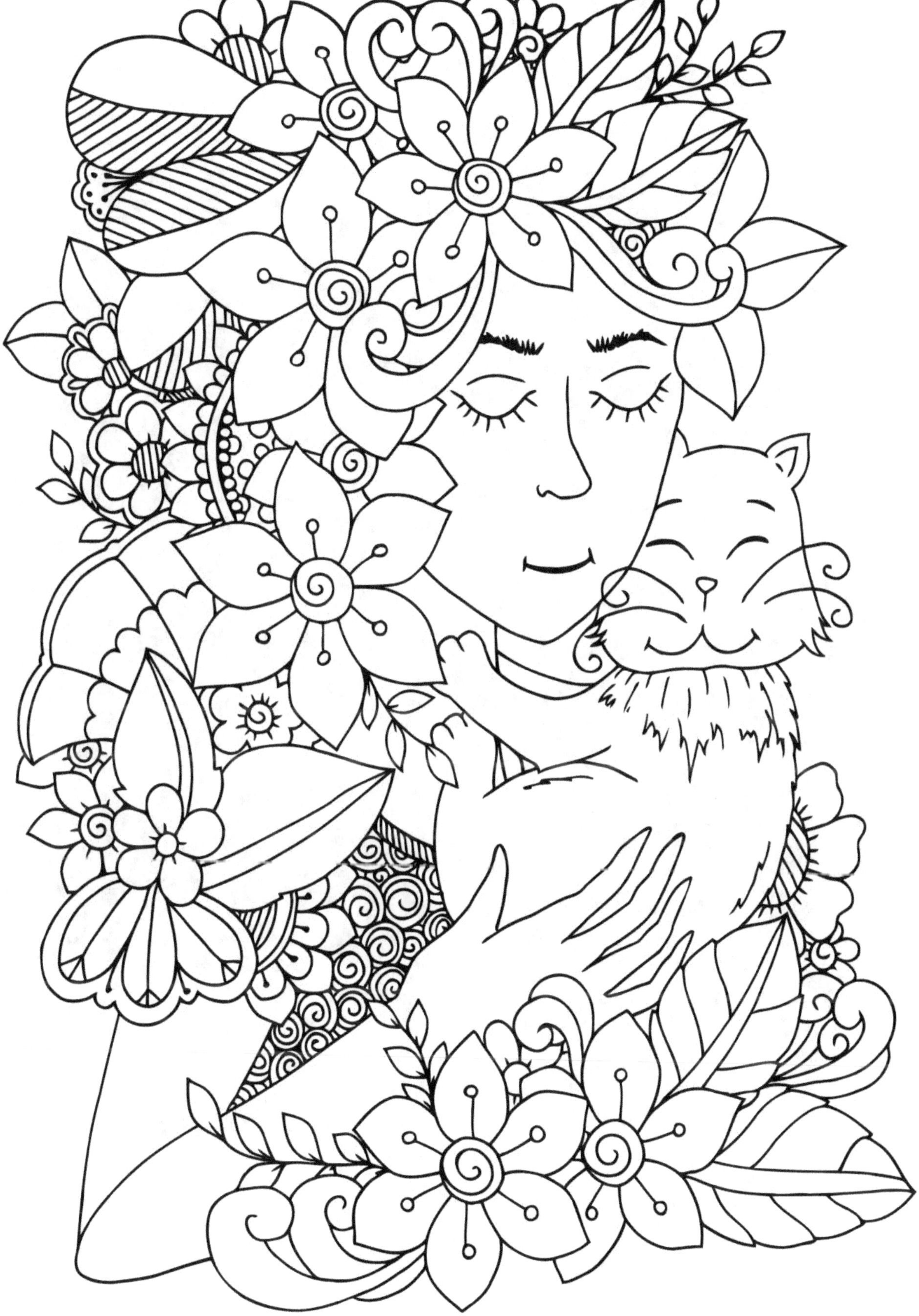

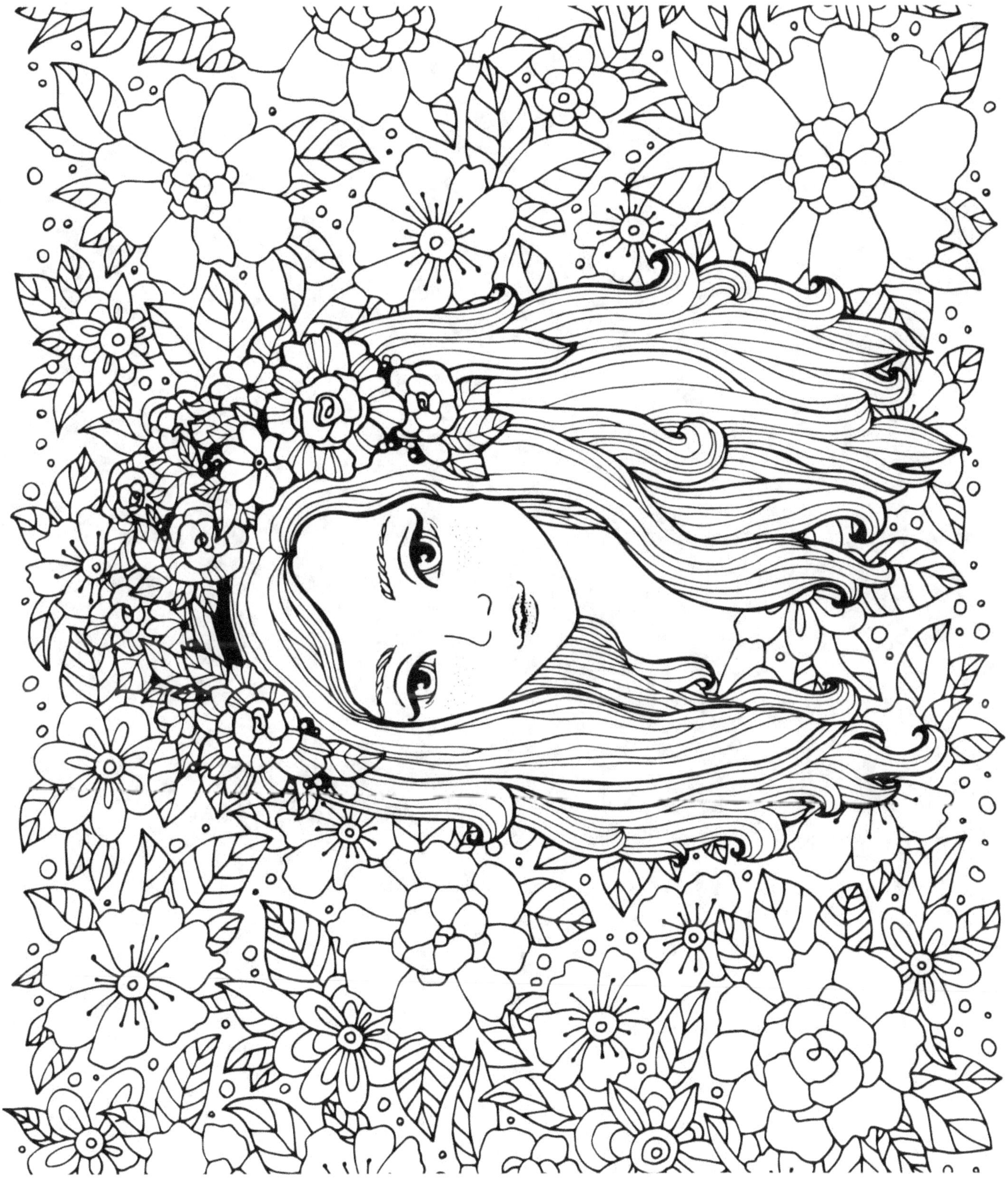

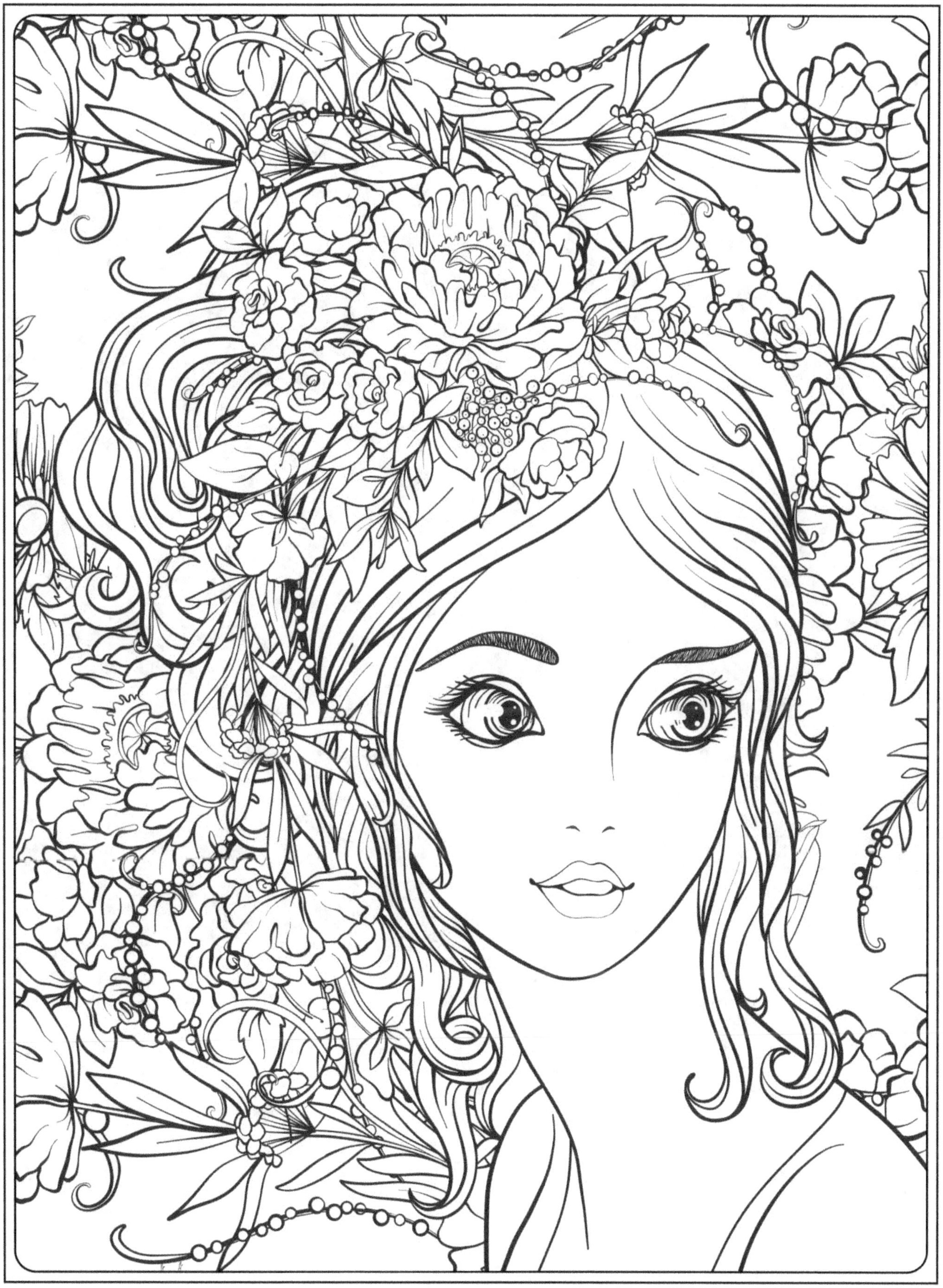

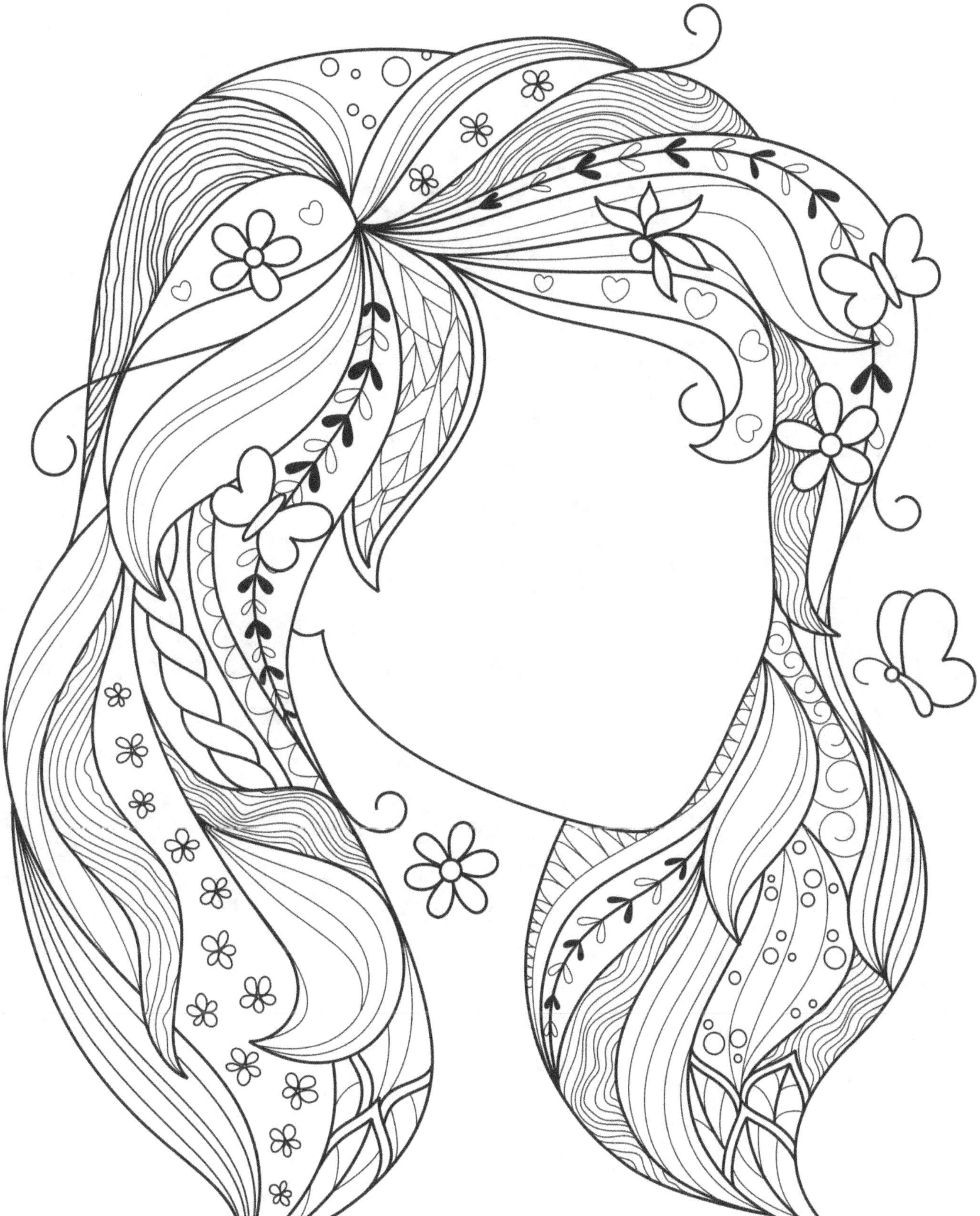

www.ingramcontent.com/pod-product-compliance
Lightning Source LLC
Chambersburg PA
CBHW081619220526
45468CB00010B/2953
* 9 7 8 1 9 7 4 5 1 6 0 4 9 *